Poems

Of

Love,

Life

&

Loved Ones

Mavis ThePathWriter

& Kawayne GodisReal

Poems of Love, Life & Loved Ones

By Mavis ThePathWriter

& Kawayne GodisReal

Unless otherwise indicated, Bible quotations are taken from New International Version. Copyright © 1987 by the Zondervan Corporation. The King James Version is also used.

Other book by Mavis ThePathWriter

(Poems of Praise Power & People)

DEDICATION

∞

I am called by God to write to His Glory
Confirmed by His Word Psalms 45:1
I have answered the call and obeyed the calling
Therefore I now dedicate this book back to God.

Thus, my readers,
I believe therefore I speak
With the authority invested in me
That as you read through this book
Dark places will come to light,
Dead areas will come to life and live.
The oppressed and depressed will be delivered.
The discouraged will be encouraged
The lost will come to the knowledge of God,
Because the words on these pages are ALIVE!!
If you believe then you will receive.

I close this dedication by speaking
To the four winds of the earth
I say,
"Breathe on these books
And take them all over the world, especially
To the hearts that need them the most Amen"!!!

ACKNOWLEDGEMENT

∽✑

I would like to acknowledge my two
sons, Rickardo and Kawayne.
Rickardo my youngest who does
some graphic designing did my logo.
Kawayne my oldest is also a writer like his mom.
Ten of his poems are added in this book.

My parents **Mr. Melbourne** and **Mrs. Olive Brown** are
my back up team. A big thank you to both of you!!!

Diane Lakner is just awesome she came to my home
and shows me how to set up the whole thing plus
proof reading to get my book published. Without her
I probably would be still just starring at my computer.
Thank you Diane may your blessings increase.

Thank you **Pastors Stephen** and **Janice Strader** for
acknowledging the God given gift of writing within
me. The poem FATHER and IN MEMORY of ARLENE
STRADER were both written because you put a
demand on the gift, that is awesome!! Thank you also
for allowing me to share my gift at Church.

Estela Sabeniano, **Bable Johnson** and **Amanda Wray** are *always* in my amen corner. When they have knowledge of my endeavors they are always supportive and are busy cheering me on. Thank you guys you are awesome friends.

In good times or bad time I can *always* call on **Sis. Margaret Mathis** and her husband **Henry Mathis**, they are my second parents.
Miracle Temple is the first Church I went to after leaving Miami. **Carlotta** and hubby **Greg Mathis**, thank you **all**, grateful am I that God should bless me with a second family.

As iron sharpens iron, so one man sharpens another Pr.27:17. It matters not the length of time or how far in between I have a conversation with **Sis Annette McDaniel**. I am always sharpened in the things of God. Kudos to you my friend you are extremely appreciated. Thank you!!!

INTRODUCTION

∞

T his is my second book and I believe this is a great time to answer a few questions asked by readers and listeners of the poems God has blessed me with.

"Where do you get the words to write your poems?" Is a question asked several times. I am a Christian inspirational writer and they aspire from a relationship with Jesus. Then someone else would ask, "When and how do you get inspired?" To that I would say, "Any time and many ways." Sometimes inspirations are stoked while I read the Bible, at times when I face obstacles and when I ask the Lord a question the answer would come in a poetic form.

I try to have a pen and paper everywhere I go, since many poems start with an idea. When I say start does not necessarily means the first line since the thought or idea could be for the middle or the last line of the poem. Sometimes others would request me to write, yet I would still have to wait on the anointing and the flow to write, several of these types are written in acrostic form.

God's ways are limitless when it comes to inspiration. Sometimes I write after being sensitive to others hurt, frustration and pain. I could literally feel their struggle and weariness and my outlet is writing to get a relief. It is even a greater joy and amazement to watch others get a breakthrough, as they read what God put on my heart for them.

In one instance The Lord showed me a video (In the spirit) I would say on about 13inch TV screen, of a mother getting herself and children ready for Church. It was chaotic and hilarious at the same time, I was laughing as I watched. When it was over The Spirit of the Lord said, "Write what you saw," My son Rickardo believes that poem is a classic. My focus is to share with you a few different avenue of inspiration (since the overall is vast).

While working in the health field in Miami I had a patient that I was taking care of on a one, to one basis. I met her seamstress since I was the one who took her each time she went. One day the seamstress ask me to stop by on my way home to pray for her because she was depress and was having a hard time going to sleep. While I was driving to her house I ask the Lord what Bible verse I should (quote) when I prayed for her since several were on my mind. The Lord told me to recite a particular poem for her. I obeyed and she got her deliverance instantly and was praising God.

These poems are alive, open your hearts and let them touch your life as the Lord leads.

One of my greatest joys and zeal is to recite the poems God blessed me with. In another case I remember stopping and reciting poems for some young men that were landscapers and elevator operators on my way to another job in Miami. God's anointing would saturate the place each time I recited the poems and now I know why they use to call me, "The Spirit Lady".

POEMS of LOVE, LIFE & LOVE ONES have *four sections.*

    LOVE (section one) Gives a glimpse of the depth and height of God's love for us, also the open door as we return that love.

    LIFE (section two) focus on the importance of us being obedient so we can fullfill our purposes in life.

    LOVED ONES (section three) are poems written to honor, loved ones, men/women of God, family, and friends.

    KAWAYNE'S POEMS (section four) are poems written by my oldest son Kawayne. I add these poems to encourage him, and to bless you the readers. Also hoping it will boost him to write more and publish his own book.

CONTENTS

<u>LOVE</u>

(Part One)

LIFE

(Part Two)

LOVED ONES

(Part Three)

<u>KAWAYNE'S POEMS</u>

(Part Four)

Love

Part One

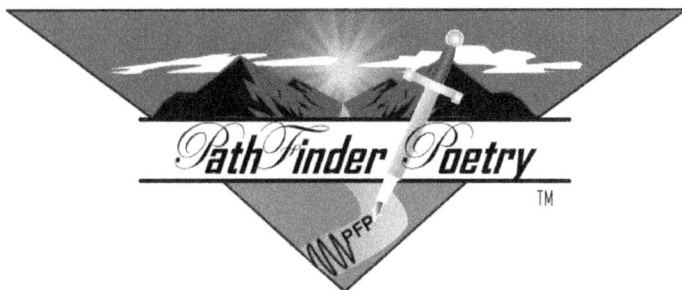

A TAMED HEART

Once I have loved, loved hard and deep
Yet the other party did not want to keep
My heart and uncaringly just played around
Break it into many pieces and tossed it to the ground.

Shell shocked, despondent, hurt and feeling used
Unwanted, betrayed, rejected, emotionally bruised.
I promise myself to keep my heart in an iron cage
"Never will I love again!!" I said in wild rage.

But Jesus You has won me,
And my whole being is filled with love
Flowing from Your River of living water above.
This is forever your desire from the very start.
And now I love again, because Jesus
You TAMED MY HEART.

JUST CHECKING

At times I say, "Abba!!"
Yet not to ask for a thing.
Wanting You close, and this way,
Checking the connection string.

Knowing if I don't hear You,
Or feel Your presence,
Does not mean You are gone.
Believing Your promise,
Never will You forsake us,
Or leave us alone.

So each time I say, "Abba!!" is more saying,
"I love You", More than just mere checking!!!

SMILE

Greet The SONshine with a smile
Though darkness has been for more than a while.
Show appreciation with the heart of a child
Know that Jesus is with you, every yard and mile.

Even though the road is rough
The rain has fallen yet the dirt still tough.
Don't get vexed and huff and puff
Know that God knows, when enough is enough.

STILL WATERS

In You dear Lord are all my fountains
Even the springs that trickle down the mountains.
You refresh me with Your waves
Of Your ocean of love, I am en-slave.

You restore and rule
Over all my surging seas.
When anxiety swells up,
Like a bubbling brook
You calm me.

From Your streams
You quench the thirst of
Your sons and daughters.
And feed us beside lakes of quiet,
Peaceful, still waters.

Jesus you are the well, sitting on the well
Now that we're filled with rivers of joy, we'll go tell
The world that You are a reservoir that is endless
Filled with love that is matchless.

BUT YOU WOULDN'T LET ME

I had it all planned out
A list of things to worry about.
I prepare a chair in front of a table
Set up the scene, yet I was not able
To worry, because You wouldn't let me.

You tap my shoulder and say,
"You won't worry today."
Though I change seat thrice You
Followed and say, "No way."

Then I said,
"Since You don't want me to I will not!!"
Your love and determination
Over took me and I did not
Worry, because You wouldn't let me.

I can't remember what it was about
Why I got all upset and started to pout.
Yet I remember planning not to smile but to be sour
Yet my little plan for the day, did not last an hour
Because You wouldn't let me.

That morning as I drove to work,
right in front of my car
Were two little birdies having a tug-a-war

Back and forth they pull each other
With a piece of string
I burst out laughing,
This is the first I've seen such a thing
I didn't pout all day, because you wouldn't let me.

As soon as I got saved, I started to think of my past
Of who done me wrong and how to get even at last.
Now that You are with me and You are my Source
To avenge me of my enemies with Your great Force.
But You wouldn't let me.

You would not let me
Remain ignorant of satan's device
You told me, "To live in unforgiveness,
Is too big of a price"
You teach me to release
It to You, which is the right way.
And I humble myself and give in, and say
"Thank You, I don't have a bitter heart,
Because You wouldn't let me."

SUGARY FAITH

In our daily diet,
We need to watch what we eat.
Being balance in our intake,
So we will be healthy, not living in defeat.

But for praise and worship,
The proportion we need not watch.
Because a dose of sugary faith,
Is all we'll catch.

ADDICTED

∞

Addicted.......Yet to what I wonder
In need of this, or that, to what I ponder?
Feeling down in the dumps yet knowing I am bless
Waking up from an eight hour sleep yet feeling stress.

Restless and hungry, yet not sure for what
Making a sandwich, yet knowing I didn't need that.
In another room on the radio I heard some praise
Then the light bulb came on, I did not do this for days.

I rush in that room with my hands upraised
Trying to catch up, praise so hard, It seem I was dazed.
Then the weight of this world rolled off my shoulder
My eyes flew open to what happen as I got bolder.

Getting my praise and worship on, all in the mix
Then all was well, renewed after getting my praise fix.
So if you see me getting my praise on,
Don't be offended.
Hands swaying, head bobbing,
Thankfulness blended.

Just trying to satisfy what I love and crave
For adoration and giving glory to God I am a slave.
Fully persuaded that if taken to court, I'd be convicted
That to praise and worship, I am addicted.

FOR YOU AND WITH YOU

Early in the morning we seek Your face
Then You bless us with Your mercy and grace.
Our spirit reaches out for You at noon
And Your sweet presence causes our heart to
Efflorescence and bloom.

We wait patiently for You in the evening
Then we feel sad when we thought You were leaving.
Our soul yearn for Your aura at night
We pursue Your delight at twilight.

When we realize that without You we were restless
Then our search for You became relentless.
And we surrender to Your desire,
No more mere visitation
Here we are Lord, twenty four seven,
We want Your habitation.

PROVE TO ME YOU LOVE ME,
BY TAKING CARE OF YOU

God is concern about us, in every way
He lovingly watches over us, each and every day.

He doesn't exasperate us by always looking for flaws
And just when we think He is all about rules and laws.

Then He softly whispers~~~~
"Prove to Me you love Me....by taking care of you."

THE LION'S CUB

Jesus The Lion of the tribe of Judah
Not Mohammed, Selassie or Buddha
The True Vine from which I bud
I am not The Lion but I am The Lion's cub.

YOU ARE WHAT LOVE IS

Jesus You are my desire
And You set my soul on fire
You are the air that I breathe
God's Word that I read.
You are what love is.

Jesus You are life, You are light
You open our eyes and give us sight
You redeem us from the hand of our foe
And direct us in the way we ought to go.
Because You are what love is.

You encamp in the depth of our being
In every fiber of our life, may You be seen
Because You are the song that we sing
Lord You are our everything.
You are what love is.

You break down gates of bronze for us
And cut through bars of iron, You are glorious
We'll stand in the congregation and praise Your name
Because You deliver us from sin, and bury our shame.
You are what love is.

With boughs in hands, we'll join the festal procession
On the throne of our hearts sits our only Possession.
Worshiping You is our obsession
Leading us into secret places is Your profession.
Yes!! You are what love is.

Lord we are Your choir
Taking us deeper taking us higher
Setting our souls ….on fire
Stretching us is Your desire.
Because You are what love is.

THE REDEEMED

Jesus the High Supreme
Who has delivered us from all schemes
And now we're highly esteemed
So let the liberated declare, "I am redeemed."

He has taken our retribution
And gave us instead salvation
Bought with a price, which is His sacrifice
Let the redeem of the lord rejoice.

Our sighing has turned into singing
And freedom bells are now ringing
Sorrow had to flee, tears turn to glee,
Let the free, unchained legs, dance merrily.

Water had gushed forth from our wilderness
Once cowards, we are now brave and fearless.
Crown with joy are those that were restless
And the ransomed of the Lord is filled with gladness.

The burning sand has become pools,
Of living waters, open eyes see rules as tools
As God's request, for us to progress and then attest
That we are the redeemed of the Lord
And we're blessed.

TOO WEAK TO WALK

∞

When life difficulties cause us to be weak
God the Father we should seek.
Time to humble ourselves and pray
Practicing these attribute each and every day.

When our feet are weary He bless us with wings
So we can fly above, opposition and things
Above hurt, pain and above offence
Above being overprotective and too much defense.

Above repression, and rejection
Above overindulgence and obsession.
Above worrying about unpaid bills
Above sickness and all ills.

So no matter what the situation and the problem
We serve a God that is awesome.
Let us pack up our troubles all in a pack
Give them to God and don't take them back.

And when we are too weak to walk, God will let us fly
On our knees we grow wings then gravity we defy
After a while we will upgrade from flying to soaring
No flapping of wings, effortlessly gliding and touring.

NOT A WORD SAYS HE

On the Mount of Olives He agonized as He prayed
With a kiss from His friend, He was betrayed.
Bound after being seized and arrested
Then by the disciples He was deserted.
Yet not a word says He.

Chief Priest, elders, the false accuser count was large
Yet not defending Himself from one single charge.
Knowing His mission, it was for this He came
He bore all that was written, even the shame.
And not a word says He.

They mocked Him; blind folded Him
And in His face spit
Then say, "Prophesy who hit You?"
As they struck Him with their fist.
In front of sinful men a perfect man, condemn to die
Even though the foundation was lies.
Yet not a word says He.

On His back He received many lashes
Many look on, as His blood splashes.
He foreknew that by His stripes, we would be healed
In the Old Testament, this prophesy was revealed.
Therefore naught says He.

He spoke up, for the thief on the cross
Even for those crucifying Him,
Because they were lost.
He said, "God forgive them,
They know not what they do."
But for Himself He put up no defense,
Not a word or two.
Not a word for Himself says He.

He could've called thousands of angels
To take Him down
Down from the cross where He was bound.
Because it was not the nails that held Him there
But stays for us that He loves and care.
So to the angels, not a word says He.

So let us remember this, when we get defensive
And put our dukes up, when others are offensive.
Pilate tries to release Him
But He was at no one's mercy
So let's stay still when tempted to get in controversy.
And sometime naught says we.

FAVOR

We thank You, God, for favor
This astounding gift from our Savior.
Favor with You and with man/woman
This vast blessing, since this world began.

Favor is ours because we're Your offspring
Which stir Your goodness, even from within.
Your favor has also woo us, away from sin
Though undeserved, this will cause us to win.

Favor will lift us up and cause us to soar
Your favor will even open for us closed doors.
And more, since for your children it's not rare
Favor is not reasonable, favor is not fair.

Favor is unmerited, favor is not earned
Favor is not justifiable, You give, yet it's not learned.
Favor at times causes promotion, the spurned reign
Thanks for blessing us, let it shower down like rain.

HE ASK FOR ALMS AND GOT LEGS

A cripple man sat at the gate beautiful to beg
Though he asks for alms he got legs.
That could leap, jump and run
Praising God the Father and His begotten Son.

The disciples have told him,
Silver and gold we have naught
But in the name of Jesus rise up and walk.
This amazes the people that were standing around
And the astounding miracle causes them to believe
In Jesus, and in Him Salvation was found.

ZACCHAEUS STOOD TALL

He ran ahead of the crowd
And climb a sycamore tree.
This was his stepping stone,
So the Savior he could see.
He did not miss his moment
Just because of his height
Determined that destiny shouldn't be treated slight.

Even though pint size
He stood tall in Jesus sight.
When he gave back all he
Swindle to turn wrong to right.
Many thought it was wrong
For Jesus to dine with a sinner
But Christ is sent for the lost
And Zacchaeus was transformed to be a winner.

I AM THE ONE YOU ARE LOOKING FOR

Here I am knocking at your heart door
Desiring for you to know Me and so much more.
I patiently wait, yet you won't let Me in
Even though I am He, the One that forgives sin.
I'm The One you're looking for

I see you restless and unable to sleep
Popping pills and later counting sheep.
I am He, Yahweh, Shalom, The Prince of Peace
It is Me, In Me you can find comfort and ease.
I am He; I am The One you're looking for.

The empty place in your heart is for Me
I created you, can't you see, that I am He?
I am for you, not against you, I am He that love thee
When your eyes are open, you will see that I am He.
The One you're looking for.

I hear you calling My Name, but in vain
You know, like swearing when frustrated or in pain.
Yet I reach beyond that and love you just the same
A relationship with you is My Passion and aim.
I am He; I am The One you're looking for.

You keep searching for answers that only I can give
Will peeking into crystal ball, teach you how to live?
I know the former things and the things to come
I will bring the best out of you, I know the outcome.

I am He, The One you're looking for

I see you looking for love and end up being used
Searching for a friend and wind up being abused.
Why waste your time, with that ole dynamite
For you I died, then rose again and I win the fight.
I Am The Love you're looking for

I am The Alpha and The Omega,
The Beginning and The End
The Redeemer, The Good Shepherd
El Shaddai, your Everlasting Friend.

I am Yahweh, The Only Way,
I am The Truth and The Life
I am The Messiah, The Son of God,
The Son of Man, and I am The Light.
I am The One you're looking for

I am Omnipresent, Omnipotent,
Omniscient; I am The First and The Last
The Champion of Love,
The Mighty Councilor,
With my life I paid the cost.

I am The I Am, The Amen, I was,
I am, and I am also The One to come
The Lord is My name,
Invite My Spirit in you so that you can overcome.
You need Me and I am He,
The One you are looking for.

LIFE

Part two

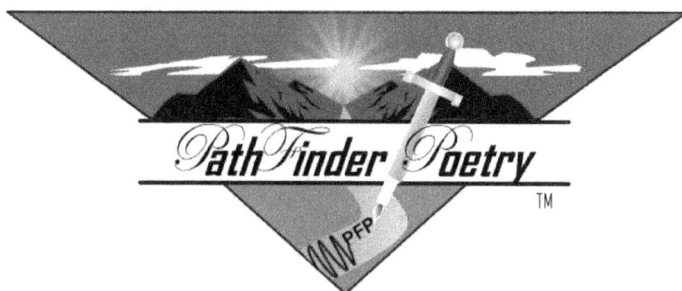

CAN YOU STILL SAY, "GOD IS GOOD"

When good things happen to us
We be smiling, no one fuss.
Promotion on the job
A good report from the lab.
Then we say, "God is good!!"

Plenty of food on the table
Our belly is full, God is able
Can we do the same when things are tight?
Displaying a good attitude and be upright?
Can we still say, "God is good?"

One day everything might be great
The next all seem to deteriorate
Will we change our mind about God?
One day He is good, the next He is bad
In difficult times can we still say, "God is good?"

If we focus on the good things as security
And the bad as obscurity
Then the transition will caused us to shift
Let us learn and not turn from God during the twist
Because God is good.

We are unique but our situation is not rare
And someone else has the problem we share.
And know that God will let even the bad
Work for our good, because He is an awesome Dad.
*Because God is **always** good.*

41

STINKING THINKING

∞

Stinking thinking dirties up the mind
Sometimes leads to actions that are way out of line.
When a thought is negative don't rehearse it
Neither nurse it, or converse it,
But instead reverse it!!

Then think on what is honest, true, pure and just
On what is lovely; a good report you can trust.
Cast down stinky thoughts,
Since they hurt us and some lead to sin.
Bad actions start from what
We reminisce from within.

Worry is liability thinking, this will steal our joy
Wasted moments so deceptive and so ploy.
Don't settle for less, God has given us this gift
To choose what we think about
And we can make a shift.

He equip us with His Spirit,
Of Power, Love and Sound Mind
To destroy satan's evil thoughts,
So we won't be blind.

Let us be alert, read our Bible
And feed our brain good food.
Let's think what we're thinking about,
Since it tones our mood.

Revengeful thinking is
When unforgiveness sets in.
If we hang onto grudges,
This way we just can't win.

Self is hurt when we meditate
On what destroy the mind.
So let it go and let God take care of it,
In His own time.

Thoughts travel like birds, that we can't stop,
From flying over our heads.
But we can stop both from nestling there,
And making their beds.

So let us renew our mind and think on
What are virtuous and with praise.
Thinking on wholesome thoughts today,
Tomorrow and all of our days.

NO TIME

"No time, no time, no time," we say
No time to read the Bible, no time to pray.
I have time for my electronic gadget,
Things that make me stray.
Time is just too short;
We need more hours in a day.

Busy checking our emails
And updating our face book page.
Upgrading our this and that,
Keeping up with the new age.
I am busy watching TV,
I am with my IPod.
I am busy making more money,
Yet I have no time for God.

Busy doing my exercise,
Can't you see I'm flexing?
No time for face to face conversation,
Yet we have time for texting.
For the things we want to do,
We will even make time.
Whatever makes us happy,
Whatever makes us chime.

Though in Church,
My cell phone is on,
God no time for You.
My mind is on my boyfriend/
Girlfriend, I mean my boo.
Yet in the time of tragedy
Everybody asking God,
"Where have you been?"
You should be busy protecting us,
Even when we are preoccupied doing our thing.

If we do not put God first,
Whoever/ whatever is, that is our idol.
That which reign on the throne
Of our heart, sitting there like a rival.
What we sow, that we will reap,
What we invest into, will be our gain.
Yet always putting God first,
Should always be our aim.

LIFE DOES NOT, COME ON A PLATTER

Life does not come on a platter,
Instead on a fragile paper plate.
So let us give it a good foundation,
Before it's too late.
To deal with spills, leaks,
We need a source that is Higher.
So let us begin each day with daily prayer.

Because when we put God first,
Because Him we choose.
Know the sand is too
Great a number for us to lose.
Great sailors are not made by smooth seas.
But prayer in times of difficulties,
And faith in God, are the keys.

The best way to be
Prepared for life, is to Pre-Prayed.
It's important to talk to God
Before we start out each day.
Practicing this, then teaching it
To our sons and daughter.
So even in hard times, we
Can be filled with laughter.

Poems of Love, Life & Loved Ones

SWEET TOOTH

Let us be careful of our sweet tooth
>>>>The sins that we love
Because what we think is candy
>>>>A Treat
Might be a be Trick
>>>>Temptation
That leads to cavity
>>>>Sin
Then tooth extraction
>>>>Death.

(Romans 6:23)
The wages (payment) of sin is death
But the free gift of God is eternal life
Which is in The Christ Jesus.

IF YOU HAD WALK A MILE IN MY SHOE

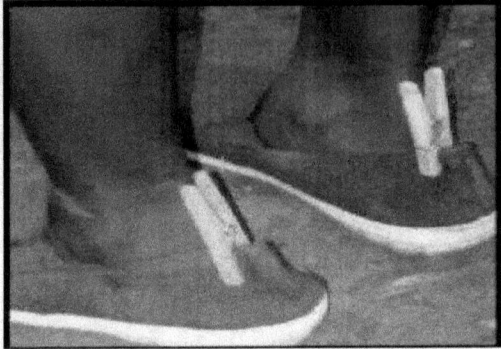

Excited about my testimony, telling what God gave
You said I act as if I am the only one God has saved.
If you had encounter what I have at first hand
Then of course you would understand.
Cynical because you didn't walk a mile in my shoe.

You invited me to your birthday party,
I thought it would be fun since we're both yardie.
Yet plan to protect my weakness, as I should.
"Heavenly minded no earthly good," You said
Because you didn't walk a mile in my shoe.

Sometimes I just praise the Lord with all my might
Yet you look down at me, as if my action isn't right.
Well, probably for you it don't take all of that
Yet more dirt needs more cleaning and that is what.
You would understand if you walk a mile in my shoe.

At your visit, you gasp as you enter my door
You ask, "For a worshiper why are you so poor?
You should have everything in galore"
You forgot you came to reap from me and more
Being critical since you didn't walk a mile in my shoe.

I have offended you with my shouts of Halleluiah
You wanna know what is going on with me and Yah.
Please know that is a sign of gratitude
And to my Lord that is the right attitude.
Zeal would not offend you,
If you walk a mile in my shoe.

Much is expected from whom much is given
My troubles have been many,
And much have been forgiven.
So say what you want..... Mock all your mock
Look down at me I won't take stock.

Because if you experience all I have been through,
You will understand my wild praise......because you
***have** walked a mile in my shoe.*

USED

We think unfavorably when we hear the word used
Broken people, tears, rejection, shame, and abused.
Hurt, pain, kicked to the curb, unwanted, confused
Many stay away from users, no one like to lose.

Even with things the unscratched we would choose
Checking fruits, vegetable when buying produce.
The untouched and fresh is considered the best
So use things and love people, so we can be blessed.

But let's turn the table and give the word used a test
Because people use people but God do what is best.
If we use people it degrades them
And cause great dishonor
But when God uses us it removes
The shame and gives us great honor.

SPIRITUAL HEALING

Many seek doctors because of all kind of ailments
From all kind of pain, all kind of assailment.
Sometimes not sure if it's psychological
Or physical since it's all in the mix
End up with prescribe medicine, that can't fix.
Can't fix, because they need spiritual healing.

Sin sick souls, need no pills,
Instead God's will, which is Salvation
Written in the Bible, from Genesis to Revelation.
Many spiritually blinded, knows not, Jesus is the cure
The answer to their many questions, and much more.
We all need spiritual healing.

Un-forgiveness can cause spiritual obstruction
Which leads to anxiety, and all kind of sensation.
Some try to dance over it, with music and humor
Temporally help, then back to being a gloomer.
Forgiveness is a part of spiritual healing.

People problems causes physicians to be puzzled
Sometimes listless, and sometimes bamboozled.
Everything has its place, exercise, diet and more
Yet there are certain times these are not the cure.
Sometimes we need Spiritual healing

How can aspirin fix your emotion?
Can it replace God? It is time for devotion.
Can medicine deliver you from demon possession?
Can pills mend a broken heart and oppressions?
For these we need God's healing.

Liquor, drugs, nicotine, and sex
Is NOT the answer for a barren soul
Not for that empty spot in our heart,
Always put God in control.
Our Creator is the only one that can make us whole.
He made us; He knows our contents and knows best.
We need Him; He should not be just a guest.
We all need spiritual healing.

Spiritual healing, is a faith base medical field
To God, our spirit, soul and body must we yield.
Who treats the ailment and not just the symptoms
So we can be at peace, grow in Him, and blossom.
For this to happen, we need to go to God for healing.

AMBASSADOR

An ambassador, representative, epitome of another
An official who acts as an extension of the leader.
High rank, they negotiate, supporting the sender
In alignment with the mission, like a super- intender.

As people of God, we are ambassadors of Christ
Representatives of the Messiah, agents of light.
Delegates, chosen vessel, carrying the good news
Illustration of Jesus on earth, we are His crews.

Peculiar, means we're unique, distinct and special too
Pilgrims in this world, we are just passing through.
As intercessors we stand in the gap for others
Mediators, and deliberators, the will of The Father.

Authorized and deputized to do the work for The King
We can't afford to be weary, to perseverance we cling
Not lowering our standard, instead we raise the bar
Tactful, diplomatic, against satan we declare war.

In the Word of God we find our true identity
Recognized with Christ, are our real authenticity.
Giving homage to Jesus, our deputy, by how we act
Not embarrassment, knowing His Word are true facts.

LIVE WITHIN YOUR MEANS

We owe it to no one, to keep up with the Joneses
To be conquered by possession, God's word opposes.
Why try to live a fat man's life, on a thin man's salary?
Living in proportion with our income is satisfactory.

Sometimes we have to make our money stretch
Staying away from situations that are farfetched.
Why spend money on trifling stuff,
While children suffer from hunger?
We can set priority straight, stay away from blunder.

Not consumed by designer clothes and name brand
Be wise shoppers, make a budget, shop with a plan.
It's not written, that we should rob Peter to pay Paul
Taking from one to pay another is not a budget at all.

Buy more with money at hand, not credit card
Paying a high interest rate, make life even more hard.
As it is written, the borrower is a slave to the lender
Owe no one, but only to love them,
Should be our only agenda!

GENEROSITY

Generosity is a condition of the heart.
This attribute can be seen in a child,
Even from the start

That open handedness,
Kindness, that willingness to give freely
Cast your bread upon the water,
And it will come back to you liberally.

Giving can be sacrificial,
Especially when there is no excess
To furbish others, on self, at times we
Have to spend less.

All who gives generously;
Will always have more than those who hoard.
And if you're not traveling on the charity boat,
Please step aboard.

FORGIVENESS

Forgiveness is giving up your rights to get even
Like in the book of Acts~~~~the action of Stephen.
Releasing the perpetrator refusing to carry a grudge
Vengeance belongs to God; let Him be the final judge.

Unforgiveness can cause sickness and desease
An open door for satanic attack, and life lack of ease
Vindictiveness affect us physically,
Spiritually and emotionally
We can maintain ourselves, by forgiving willingly.

Conflict is inevitable, but combat is optional
Whether it is at home, next door, or international.
Forgiveness does not excuse others bad behavior
Yet, stay free from plotting, the example is our Savior.

JUST DO IT

Don't flap your flappers
About what happened.
Save your energizer
Battery, to do what you got to do.

Why make a big hullabaloo
About what you still will have to do.
Conserve your livener
To do what need to be done.

Some don't want situations to be fixed
So they can get clack and flap in the mix.
Yet this is the way to blew it,
When you just slam dunk and **JUST DO IT.**

DID YOU REALLY MOVE OUT?

For so long you seemed so stuck
Then I saw the moving truck.
You know My Word yet you were shacking
And when he started to abuse you, you went packing.

But yet the question still arise, "Did you really move?"
Because only then, who I have for you can I approve.
But I can't, since your heart is still there
Listen! I want you to really move out my dear.

A PROPHETIC SOUND

I hear a sound
Then I put my ear to the ground
It's a thundering sound
The sound of hoofs
Yea riders are coming
They are for me
They are not against me.

They have a spare horse
Saddle up mama/papa
No fooling around
Because they won't stop
When they get to you
So feel the momentum
Feel the rhythm and beat
Gear up!! Cheer up!!

And when they get to you
Leap on your horse
The spare one that is for you
And ride on.
This is no pony express
This is from God
Join the team
And ride on……..
SWOOSH>>>>>

THE SINS THAT WE LOVE

The sins that we hate are no threat
Yet the sins that we love can cause premature death.
These are the ones we keep close to our bosom
Feed and nourish them until evil blossom.

Even though it might be hard we need to let them go
Let God fill that spot in our heart and let His love flow.
The enemy of our soul comes to kill, steal and destroy
So let us denounce all sins, not treating them like a toy

A chain is as strong as the weakest link
And hating all sins is the way to stay away from kinks.
So in our daily lives let us all take heed
Trusting and obeying God is the way to succeed.

THE PIG PEN

Once there was a man who had two sons
The youngest asked for his portion,
From his father's funds.
The kind hearted father,
Though broken hearted, heeded his request
This son took his entire portion and went on his quest.

He squandered all his inheritance, on riotous living
Then realized it was not what he thought,
The empty life he was craving.
When his money was gone, all his company disperse
And even though blessed, he was living under a curse.

No one gave him anything,
Not even his so-called friends
So in lack he ends up feeding swine, in the pig pen.
The light bulb came on, that's when realty hit
Then he came to himself,
In the pig pen, he no longer sits.

He went back to be a servant,
Who are well fed in his Dad's house
His Dad accepts him as a son, showing
Him what unconditional love is about.
He returned meek, not demanding
The rights of a fallen son.

Now humbled, because rebellion
Is where the trouble had begun.

In the pig pen,
This young man sure
Did learn his lesson.
By seeking the fast things in life,
He had ran away from his blessing.
In the pig pen wisdom speaks and he sure did listen.
It says, "Not everything is good,
Just because it glistens."

In the pig pens,
Is where most will admit they have a problem
And some will humble and listen at rock bottom.
A very few if any will come to God
When life is hunky- dory.
Yet when He forgives us and helps us,
We end up giving Him the Glory.

WHEN DESTINY MEETS PASSION

Our destiny is our purpose,
Who God has called us to be.
That calling intended beforehand,
The Master divine decree.
Each assignment has obstacles,
Sometimes discouragement can set in.
And that is why with it we need passion,
Which will boost us to win.

Passion is that zeal,
That desire that push, our mission to action.
The knowledge of our vision is one part,
So we need more than that fraction.
So write the vision down,
Make it plain, and prepare to walk or run.
But remember patience,
Because we need this to overcome.

Destiny will cause you to dream,
Passion will push you to cross over.
When mission seem impossible,
Passion teach you to maneuver.
Passion is that launching force,
Which motivates you to start then finish.
The gift of sacrifice, like a mentor,
That won't let duty diminish.

Let no one's jealousy abort your dream,
Let passion stir up your gift.
No matter how hard it seems,
That friendly faith on fire, will give you a lift.
If you don't know what your mission is,
Go wireless on your knees.
Having a relation with God through His Son,
That really is the key.

Be fervent in prayer,
There is an assignment to accomplish.
Let love take you higher,
It takes hard work and not a wish.
Remember, because a spring runs
Underground, does not mean that it is dry.
Let providence hang out with passion,
Because enthusiasm won't let it die.

If the dream killer tries to kill your dream,
Passion will fan it back to life.
Realize it will mobilize and
Organize your mission to thrive.
So answer the call, walk in your vocation,
Of all God call you to be.
He desire, your final destiny to be with Him,
To spend all Eternity.

THE COLOR OF ONE'S SKIN

No one should be treated
Based by the color of their skin.
Look up at; look down upon,
Instead of what dwells within.
Opportunity snatch from some,
Their skin pushes them out of season.
While some are spoiled and pampered
Their outer garment skin the reason.

In God's image we are made,
In the image of our Creator.
To walk upright on two feet
Head upright towards our Maker.
How much do we differ?
We cry, we laugh, we **all** die
What does pain have to do with color?
Don't tell me let sleeping dog lie.

People steal, rape and kill,
Which are all so very sad.
Some do good, some do bad,
Because they turn from God.
Sin which is internal, sometimes expressed external
Judge by Him who is Eternal.
Yet, God never judges, by the color
The color of one's skin.

IS SILENCE ALWAYS GOLDEN?

They say silence is golden, and then I ask,
"Why did God speak?"
Don't try to drone me out, or lullaby me to sleep.
If God call us to rise up, there is a cause
To speak up for our future generation,
Not the time for eternal pause.

Sometimes silence is a sign,
Someone have a yellow streak
Yet let it not remain that way,
When a voice, is what God seeks.
Silence can lend strength, to the force of evil
So let us speak up, and expose the devil.

Silence is golden when,
You don't know what you are talking about.
Instead of making a fool of yourself,
It is best to close your mouth.
Silence can be a teacher,
It gives an opportunity to listen
Not talking ill of others is a good way how to glisten!

It is true that some things are better off unsaid.
Yet there are other times, when silence causes
others to end up dead.

Silence could be an insult;
It could be a sign of scorn
It could be a time of wicked plan
Then evil plots are born.

Silence can give satan a field
Day, then later a play ground.
Then he laughs in your face,
When everyone is around.
At times this quote is used to
Hide evil, so others mouth is still.
And to guarantee it happen,
Some go to the extreme and kill.

Let it be known,
That we should not be silent
About things that really matter.
Because silence could mean consent,
And could be used as means to flatter.
Yet the conclusion of the matter is "balance"
Balance is what we all should seek.
Because, there is a time to be silent
***and there is also a time to speak.

WE WIN

For some of us 2016 has been a very difficult year
Lost of loved ones, sicknesses, and all kind of fears.
But despite it all, remember that God cares
And even if our back is against the wall, we can dare.
To say, "WE WIN".

2017 is the year to travel lightly, get rid of all baggage
Leaving toxic relationship behind with its luggage.
For those who love God,
This is not a year to fool around
Especially when the honor for God
Has fallen to the ground.
Yet despite it all WE WIN.

So stay in the race, 2017 is the year to climb higher
Not letting our past mess up our future,
Should be our desire.
Let's trust God even when it seems
We're pinned in a corner.
With God with us in no way we are a goner.
Therefore WE WIN.

THE ACCUSATION OF MY THUMB

I have no tolerance for
Imperfection; I'll tell it to you all.
As soon as the Church gets it together
I'll consider answering God's call.
The first Church I visit was half empty;
The second have too big a crowd.
The third had no music at all;
The fourth music was too loud.

Wooden pews cause me to blister,
The cushion seats put me to sleep.
And to add insult to injury
The pastor refer to me as sheep.
Dead Churches make me sad,
Holy rollers leave me confused.
Extravagant buildings are too much,
The dilapidated leave me bemused.

Some ministers are too demonstrative
While some speak, in monotone.
Some only preach to get money,
While the thought chill some to the bone.
Some Church folk are too friendly,
Others are downright stuck up.
Some refuse to speak while others won't shut up.

The paint on the walls is too pale
The choir robes are too bright.
Some insides are too dim
While others have too much light.
It seem I find the right the church,
Yet they seat me in the wrong pew.
And when they expect offering,
This offence just makes me blue.

Some sermons are too simple;
They leave me no room to think.
While some are too complicated,
It drives my brain to the brink.
Some Churches are too hot,
And then insult me with paper fan.
Some air condition is so freezing cold
To this day I can't understand.

Some preachers are compromising,
While others are way too strict.
Some Christians are so cheerless,
While others joy makes me sick.
Some sermons are too short,
While others are too long.
Some are diluted,
While others are just too strong.

It's difficult to get in the inner circle
The rejection is belittling.
Some expect you to work without money,

Such status is just brittling.
They make me so uncomfortable
When they preach about hell.
I don't like message about milk and honey,
Just listening make me swell.

All the Churches are full of
Hypocrites and I am not like them.
I hear the voice of God calling me,
Yet will I answer? And when?
I have no tolerance for imperfection
And I'll tell you one and all.
As soon as the Church gets it together
I will answer God's call.

Yet I have one more complain, I'll say it before I run
Every time I point my finger at the Church,
I'm being accused by my thumb.

FAILURE

∞

My name is failure; I am not nice at all
I don't want you to succeed, and I love when you fall.
I like couch potatoes, to me they are no threat
Complainers are my favorite, as you can so bet.

I am that whispering voice that tells you, you can't
My first cousin is excuses, the blame game is my aunt.
If you follow my track record, I fancy a lifestyle of sin
If you remain that way, for sure you just can't win.

Pessimist is my peeps,
They shoot themselves in the foot.
The wise feed their faiths, then get off my hook.
Those who slump in comfort zone, won't advance
I use fear to freeze many, they don't have a chance.

I have company, I follow closely behind pride
In regret, condemnation, self-hate, self pity I hide.
Some of my customers they slip away from me
Because when God gives them hope, I have to flee.

The only permanent failure, is for you to give up
Another kept secret, is to stop drinking from my cup.
I'm forced to say this, since I don't want you to gain
The only way for ME, failure to fail, is for YOU to GET
UP and try again.

YOUR WORD

May reading Your word, be our greatest delight
Allowing us to walk deeper depths,
And climb higher heights.
While we read Your word,
May they come alive and leap off the pages
So, we can learn from the patriarch,
Your people of past ages.

May Your word build our faith,
So we will not be frightened.
May they open our eyes,
So by them we will be enlightened.
By Your word,
Show us how to enjoy Your creation,
Show us how to live
And when we are provoked,
By Your word teach us to forgive.

By Your word,
May we lean on You, with no need to strain,
By Your word, may we acknowledge You,
And from all evil refrain.
By Your word,
May the treasure in us be unlocked and discovered
By Your word, may unrepented sin in us be
uncovered.

May we be known,
By Your word, because we are lively stones.
Being aware of Your presence,
Knowing we are never alone.
May we be witnesses of Your word,
And become world impacters,
By Your word may we be radicals,
And be a nothing lacker.

May we allow Your word to teach us,
And keep tempers under wraps
Be a light to our feet,
And keep us from all satan's traps.
May Your word, be the deputy of our faith
Causing us to be patient, with the right attitude,
While we wait.

May we allow Your word,
To force us out, of all bad habits
And destroy all the enemy organized scare tactics.
By Your word, may we be champions
Who know our role.
And I pray we be obedient, to Your word, so that
Heaven will be our final goal.

GO TELL

In this world there are many
Tom, Sue, Ellen and Jenny
Who does not know Christ
So let us lift our voice
As witness is our choice
To every girl and boy
Let's first dwell,
And then go tell
About the love of Jesus.

We are not Religious
And neither superstitious
Not even the-prestigious
So let's be adventitious
And be a living witness.

Of God's mercy and His goodness
Forgiveness and His kindness
Away with double-mindness
Let's first dwell, and then go tell
About the love of Jesus.

How can we be selfish?
After tasting love so precious
We can't keep this to ourselves
Or hide it on a shelf
Let's first dwell, and then go tell
About the love of Jesus.

In Christ hope is found
His grace is so profound
Salvation is so sound
Forgiveness is abound
Go spread this all around
Let's first dwell, and then go tell
About the love of Jesus.

The Gospel is no game
And we are not ashamed
To witness is our aim
And this is not for fame
Let's go now and proclaim
Let's first dwell, and then go tell
About the love of Jesus.

He feeds us
He leads us
His blessings precede us
He shields us
He keeps us
Let's dwell, and then go tell
About the love of Jesus.

Let them know
As we go and show
Them the love of Jesus
Because sharing is caring
Being bold ****is no fearing
Sometimes we got to be daring
Let's first dwell, and then go tell
About the love of Jesus !!!

No more procrastination
Rise up this is an invasion
And make the proclamation
Go tell it to all the nations
Next door*** at school,
Work and gas station
To our friends, Jews,
Gentiles, Arabs,
And Haitians.
Let's stand up
Stand out!!
Shout it out!
All about!!!
Let us first dwell
Then go tell about the love of Jesus.

MOVING RIGHT ALONG

∞

Let's not make a career out of minor problems
Neither beating a dead horse will ever solve them.
We have to walk away from some of them sometimes
Without giving it a second thought,
Not tossing it a dime.
And just move right along.

No work place politics or gossip for John
His standards are high and many don't understand,
His moral conviction. So when they try to draft him in
"I'll not sit in the seat of the scornful," He said from
within.
Then kept moving right along.

Mai' she don't like quarrels, and try to keep the peace
While some think clashing is something to achieve
So when some miserable soul tries to make a fuss
Mai' she won't argue, or make a ruckus
Saying "I got bigger fish to fry" Then move right along.

God's wisdom will teach us
Not to charade in life's masquerade
No time for trifling stuff, not joining foolery parade
Why throw pearls to swine, knowing it's a great waste
Make step one, then pick up the pace, make haste.
And move right along in the right direction.

78

DISCERNING

To be discerning is to be
Sensitive to the Holy Spirit yearning.
Not to be self rigid, but flexible
To where He's turning.

Which means at times we might plan this,
Yet He might lead us to that
A simple nudge or a slight turn of
The head to show us what's what.

God Spirit might cue us to
Speak at times or prompt us to act.
Always decent and in order,
Not out of turns, because He is tact.

Not for us to be spooky
Or snoopy, or being off the chain.
Not taken out of context,
Or complex, but in God's word remain.

Discerning is to be attentive,
To things not obvious to the naked eye.
Line upon line, precepts upon precepts
The ways of God we can't defy.

The ways of the wind we don't know,
No matter the level of our learning
But trusting God will manifest,
In the Spirit of Discerning.

To be discerning, is to be tuned,
To The Omniscient God, who knows it all.
Being flexible, and swayed by his Holy Spirit,
Who will not lead us to fall.

Instead He gives us signals, wave length,
According to our call.
Discerning, susceptible to
The Almighty should be the desire of us all.

NOT BEGGING FOR CRUMBS

Not begging for crumbs, but thanking God for bread
Believing in His promise of blessings, as His Word said.
Knowing even in difficult times, things will work out
Because we serve a God of faith, not God of doubt.

If we don't see bread, we'll be thankful just the same
Being joint heir with Christ, crumb begging is a shame.
Kings kids are not beggarly, if they know what they got
If we don't know of our blessings, we can stay in lack.

We are Your children Lord, and we ought to know
You are a God of more than enough;
You are God of the overflow.
Knowing if we have only crumbs,
We will eat it by ourselves
Yet, by us being blessed with bread,
We can share it with someone else.

We know Your intentions toward us
Are great, not for us to merely survive.
For us to take care of orphans and the
Needy, for this we need to thrive.
So here we are, Your children
Believing what Your Word said.
Sitting at Your table Lord,
Thanking You for bread.

ARISE ON EAGLE'S WINGS

Despite life's obstacles and obscurity
Mistrust, chaos on the street, protest and insecurity.
Despite harassment war and revolution
Hard times, terrorism, and persecution.
Arise!! God's people.

Arise to a higher calling
When the world thinks you are falling.
Arise when everything is appalling
Up on eagle's wings God is calling.
Arise!! God's people.

Overcoming adversity that's how we grow
Not letting the bad yeast of life ruin our dough.
Knowing the trials are the testing of our faith.
And patience is how we respond,

Not react while we wait.
Arise!! God's people.

Arise and let love shine!!
When God's word is said to be hate speech
Arise confident no fear and expand in all outreach.
Arise biblically correct and united,
Standing on holy ground.
Arise above frustration and offense
Knowing your foundation is sound.
Arise!! God's people.

Arise above prejudice,
Inferiority complex,
Negativity and depression.
Arise above the nay-sayers,
Poverty, idleness and oppressions.
Because the higher we rise the better the scenery
Above setbacks, failures, scavingerism and obscenery.
Arise!! God's people.

Arise!! Above idolatry,
Sorcery, hatred, and outburst of wrath.
Removing envy, murders, heresies,
Adultery away from our path.
Arise!! God's people.

Arise above revelries,
Lewdness, jealousy, drunkenness, and contention.
Selfish ambition, dissention, fornication
And all sins not mentioned.
Arise!! God's people

Arise!!! Arise!!! Arise!!!

LOVED ONES

PART THREE

HAPPY BIRTHDAY DADDY

Our Dad is a hard working man
Loves his children and do what he can.
To back us and boost us, and not with just mere talk
And when we are successful, he is as happy as a lark.

He proudly counts and wears us, like a badge of honor
We're thankful & wouldn't exchange him for another.
Now a Granddad and Great- Granddad,
We are the stars in his crown.
And even though we are grown,
He is not called Mr. Brown.

Even in a big crowd,
Forever and Wherever, he is still Affectionately~
"DADDY"

TO A LOVING STEP-MOTHER

∾⧟∾

A wonderful step-mother can be very rare
Yet, you are a genuine jewel, who loves and cares.
Encouraging, uplifting, and seeking to pull out the best
Out of us. These attributes mention
Are few not to mention all the rest.

We use this time to say we love you
And appreciate you too.
Hoping we all will be a blessing to you.
With love and kindness our hearts you have won.
Praying for the best and thanking you
For all you have done.

MOTHER

M-: Mentor, wise councilor, who deserves great honor

O-: Optimistic, Outstanding, a woman of great valor

T-: Tenacious, holding to what is wholesome and true

H-: Hats off to the world greatest Mom!!! We love you

E-: Efflorescent, beauty in you have been bestowed

R-: Respectfulness, Righteousness in you has showed

We love you Mom!!

A FATHER

A good father is a replica of God, right here on earth
Providing for and protecting their offspring,
Even before their birth.
A godly father train up his children,
Leading them in the way they should go.
Opening himself to the love of Jesus,
Then to his seed let this love flow.

God gives us dads to prepare us,
For a world so rough.
Some work very hard,
And their responsibility is O' so tough.
Yet with strength from God they guide,
Discipline according to their role.
Even when they are not appreciated,
And their sacrifices are untold.

A biological father is not the limit;
There are men with the heart of God.
Who father the fatherless,
And claim orphans who call them Dad.
A great father's mantle, is to lead by example,
And unashamedly following Jesus is their sample.

Pastors and leaders are fathers,
Watching out for our very soul.
They are our heroes;
We honor and respect them,
As they reach for their goal.

The greatest Father is our Heavenly Father,
Some lovingly call Him Abba.

And to all fathers
Adopted-fathers
Spiritual-fathers
Step-fathers
God-fathers
Daddy
Dada
Papa
Dad
Pa
HAPPY
FATHERS DAY!!

PRAYER FOR TODDLERS

Lord we thank You for our children
Now to You Lord Jesus, in prayer we bring them.
Please protect them while they sleep, play and run
When curiosity cause them to explore, to have fun.

Comfort them amidst
Disquieting dreams in the night.
And if they are afraid of the dark
Remind them that You are The Light.
Bless them with wisdom, understanding and health
A relationship with You, will be their greatest wealth.

TO MY DEAR CHILDREN

I am so proud of you my dear sons and daughters
You bring me delight, joy and much laughter.
I have not ceased to be amazed at how you've grown
Like a plant, from bud to blossom, from a seed sown.

Stay focused on your dreams
So in studies you know what is essential.
Not giving up, so you can reach your full potential.
Remembering always, God's word
Should not be omitted
But in Him let all you do, everyday be committed.

If obedient, as sure as spark fly upward you'll succeed
Even your mountains will turn into roads,
With the qualification to take the lead.

In many circles it might not be popular to serve God
But serve Him anyway; He is not a passing fad.
Despite life's frenzy you can remain calm.
The Creator watches over you,
To protect you from all harm.

GRAND-PARENTS SO DEAR

We thank God for our grand-parents so dear.
Thoughtful, loving and show in so many
Ways that they care.

Being so kind and good hearted
In their presence we are glad.
And very happy to know, that by them
We would be cheered up, should we ever be sad.

We know our grand-parents are the best.
And if anyone should think different
You would both pass every test.

THE FLOWERS I GIVE YOU TODAY

May the flowers I give you today,
Bring a smile to your face
And brightens your day.

Even though the flowers will fade
Or the petals might blow away.
We know the joy of Jesus
Is there in your heart to stay.

TO MY DEAR AUNT

∞

I thank God for you, my dear aunt,
Your wise counsel allows me to be like
A well nurtured plant.

You taught me that in dreams
And Agape love nothing is impossible
And showed me how to be balanced and
Extend to what seemed invincible.

These godly teachings has descended on me like dew
Changed some things in my life and made them new.
You've touched many lives
And God has seen your good deeds.
You have also trust in the Lord and He
Has supplied all your needs.

He who plant seeds, lack in their lives will be "Never"
May integrity and righteousness protect you forever.

HAPPY BIRTHDAY CARLOTTA

Happy birthday and I love you
Hoping all the desire of your heart will come through.
Respect and honor received from me, to you are due.
You are special, you are appreciated, and adored too.

Between the hearts of special friends
There is a love that never ends.
Because Agape Love conquers all things
Is a beacon in times of storms
No matter what life brings.

Happy birthday!!! I hope for you a lot of cheer
Not only for today but..year.. after year..after year..

May God bless you and your family continually*

TO MY CO-WORKERS

It is a pleasure to
Work alongside you as a team
As caring and loving the patients
Is our plan and scheme.

Your willingness to unify is appreciated,
Working with all your gusto.
Even when tired, using up all
The energy you can muster.

May you continue to be gratified each day
And the joy of completion be your final pay.

Ms. ACKER

A-: Activating the Anointing of God to bless others
C-: Caring despite life's obstacles, loving like a mother
K-: Kind, Kindred spirit, Keeper, peaceful like a dove
E-: Excellent , Empathetic, Earnest Equation of love*
R-: Righteousness that is a gift from God above*

It is awesome to watch you,
Allow God to use you, even in your difficulties.
Reaching out to others with your dolls, booties, kind
encouraging words, prayers, poems, baby clothes for
hospitals, devotions, etc. May God Bless you with
health and prosperity. Knowing that what you don't
gain here, you'll gain in Heaven.
I SALUTE YOU Ms. Vivian Ackers
Because you exemplar the love of JESUS

THANK YOU BLESSINGS

∽∾

The kind hearted gains respect
And for you, that is in many aspect.
I thank God for your godly character.
Your kindness and love shows in many factors.

Your soul will be made rich
Because of your generosity
Physically, mentally, financially
God seal of your prosperity.
Therefore your vats will be full
Overflowing with abundance.
From generation to generation
That's God's assurance.

TO A WONDERFUL COUPLE

To wonderful couple
Who have made a great difference in this life
To you man of God and your very beautiful wife.
Thank God your relationship
Is like an irremovable rock.
Because Jesus is the foundation,
Who removes all stumbling blocks.

Traveling together in depths,
Heights of adventure and discovery.
Holy matrimony with harmony and loving memories.
Continue to do special things with joy and mirth.
So that paradise and heaven
Can be right here on earth.

THANKFUL FOR GOD MOTHERS

∞

I thank God for you my dear god mother
The love you have scattered you will now gather.
Being a noble saint you make noble plans
And by your noble deeds you stand.

Always sowing your seeds beside the streams
Encouraging love ones to dream big dreams.
Your earnest support, encourage those who stumble
And words ample spoken, guide others to humble.

Being righteous you can sing and be glad
With the blessings of the Lord you are now clad.
Thank you for giving a helping hand
Because of your kindness,
You and your descendants will inherit the land.

IN HONOR of SIS VERTA MAE

We thank God for this warrior, Sis Virtue Mae
Very loyal, devoted, steadfast, dependable, each day.
Forgetting about self, standing in the gap, for others
Interceding for family also Church sister and brother.

Raging war, taking back what belongs to us
Kingdom builder, who has earned our trust
When we say she is also a praiser we aren't kidding
Focus, and attentive to do her Master's bidding.

She'll praise God when she is well, and when ill too
So hard we wonder if she will knock off her shoe.
Now we can picture her dancing up some, in Heaven
Ceaselessly, entirely, dusk to dawn twenty four seven

Sister your unanswered prayers are still alive
God has them all arrange in order in His Archive.
To perform each and every single one.
To bless all your off springs even
To the thousand generation.

IN LOVING MEMORY OF IAN BEGUESS

∞

You might have thought I have left far too young
Let faith arise and from your hurt let victory sprung.
Don't mourn for me as though without hope
Be overcome with trust, instead of to just cope.

The road on life journey has many twist and bend
Because I have gone ahead does not mean life end.
Find peace knowing God cannot make a mistake
Though on earth I sleep yet in heaven I awake.

Let the memory of me be the emblem of your love
I'm at a better place with my Father above.
Live for God so when your time comes
You can join me here.
With Jesus the Savior, the process of
Transfer has no fear.

IN MEMORY OF DOCTOR MYLES MONROE, WIFE & OTHERS

On Sunday November 9th 2014
Tragedy hit and we were in shock.
Nine precious lives taken, after
A plane hit a crane at a ship dock.
We weep, and grief,
Yet we still trust our God.
Even when we can't see the
Good that will come out of that bad.

Included was Dr Myles Monroe
Transformational Christian leader.
Globally recognized, pastor, author,

Advisor, preacher and teacher.
Who speak words that challenge,
Charge, and push us to change our conduct.
A mentor, who propel us not only to dream
But to also construct.
A great father and husband,
A positive life that emulate changing evidence.
Of God our Heavenly Father and Creator and His
Great Eminence.

God has bless us with
A wise motivator that illuminate our minds.
Doctor, apostle, conduit, of maximizing potential
And purpose, he is one of a kind.
You died living out
Purpose therefore you died empty.
With his wife a phenomenal woman,
Who is also a great example.

In this life there are
So many things we don't understand.
Yet we serve an Omniscient God and
Nothing is by happenstance.
Though your sudden departure has left us numb.
You've poured out all God gave you, leaving none.
Living your life so effectively
Therefore it will not be erased from history.

IN MEMORY OF JOYCE ARLENE STRADER

On Monday
August 11, 2014 you went to rest...
In the arms of Jesus, after living life
To the fullest, always determine to be your best.

We miss you,
Yet we know you are in a better place.
You have fought the good fight of faith, and
You have won your race.

A Proverbs 31st woman,
A wife, a mother of great honor.
Living a godly life, lifting Jesus up
Like a grand banner.

A grandmother, great grandmother,
Aunt, family, sister in the Lord and friend.
Touching many lives with notes, prayers
And love to the end.

Your life has been
A dinner bell, for many lost souls.
Thanking God for your transformational living,
That was very bold.

So go ahead, and enjoy your sweet repose our friend.
Enjoy being ahead of us, in eternity with Jesus,
Until we meet again.

GOD HAS SENT US AN ANGEL

God has sent us an angel, for yet a little while
God has sent us an angel,
Probably in the form of a child.
God has sent us an angel, which is like no other
Sometimes in the form of a sister, or a brother.
Yet, God has sent us an Angel!!!

When God send us angels it is always for a reason
Then the angel will return to God after a season.
This is very difficult for us, we cry, we weep.
Yet, our grieving hearts God will keep.
Yes, God have sent us an Angel!!!

Yet we need to know
God don't do things by happenstance.
And His desire is that we understand.
When God send us a child with special needs.
We can learn so much when we take heed.
Because God have sent us an Angel!!!

A special child teach us to be patient, we slow down
They show us to love, to smile and not to frown.
Their dependence on us cause us to learn
When we're more caring, we didn't lose but earn.
Because God have send us and Angel!!!

This angel is in Heaven, and we can take ease
Up there, there is no sickness and there is no disease.
You can join together and be a joyful family again
With Jesus in your heart and if we're born again!!!

You are missed yet we are now better people
Because God have sent us YOU an Angel !!!

USE TIME WISELY

∞

The devil thinks all is over because
You are in the slammer.
But use time wisely, read your Bible,
Use the dictionary and improve upon
Your grammar.

Listen up now
Because truth does not stutter,
Neither does it stammer.
Break sin habit down,
Let the word of God be the hammer.

KAWAYNE'S POEMS

PART FOUR

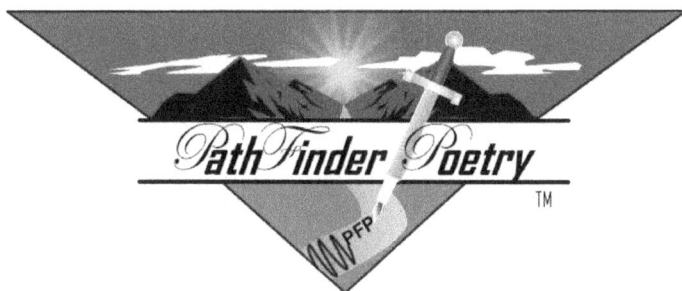

YOUR WINGS

Your Wings I can hang on, when I need a ride
Your Wings will cover me, when I need to hide.
Your Wings will be my wind, when I need breath
Under Your Wings I find comfort, there I need not fret.

Your Wings are a symbol of safety and protection
They remind me of Your greatness,
In Your Son's resurrection.
Your Wings are an emblem of Your Holy Spirit within.
Your wings Dear Lord God are my help in everything.

HUMBLE CRY

Hear my humble cry Lord; my life is full of sigh
For all I have are questions, that begins with why?
I scream out with repentance hoping nothing is amiss
My desire is for me ….not to be slipped from your list.

They say patience is a
Virtue but how long should I wait.
I'm wondering if you're listening,
I hope my cry is not too late.

All I desire
To do is to keep it real.
Hoping you will understand,
And my ways you will feel.

Even though my realness
Is like filthy rags in your sight.
I'm asking you to listen and
Turn my darkness into light.

Even in my humble cry,
I still don't feel that I am worthy.
But please listen to me Lord,
For in your ways I am sturdy.

BE

Be of song, of joy and praise
Lifting holy hands always.
Be of truth, peace, joy, delight
Find your youth in aging flight.

Be always for God in every ways,
Though life take us through many phase.
Be of the faith, past, present, future due.
No matter what the situation or the circumstances.
PLEASE BE YOU !!

GOD'S LOVE IS HERE

∽∾

God's love
Is sacred in words and deeds,
A blessing present for those in need.

To be a path that
Others can follow.
The strength for today
And faith for tomorrow.

Through trials and
Triumph God's love is clear.
It is beyond near, God's love is here.

THY READER

I remember through times
Of torment nothing could lift up my being.
But Mom poems she put on the wall for
A short time did redeem.

My inner conflict
Was controlling me I felt I was all alone.
Trying to grasp hope-
This was just a timing zone.

Could I beat it? Will this last forever?
There was nothing it seem I could do.
I then seek the Creator,
Knowing He would bring me through.
I realize everything is a God given

Privilege when I lost all control.
Of my mind, my body, it seem
My spirit and even my very soul.

However thy reader if you go through
Torment that never seems to end.
Take one moment at a time,
Daylight is around the bend.

It might not come when
You want it, but God will be on time.
Hold on to endurance
And take that experience and shine.

Just trying to give you a guide,
To relief, a way to take you through.
In the end victory will be in your hand,
For it depends on what you do.

WINK

At times nations
Over nations, rise and conquer.
Yet peace and liberty is the answer.
Like a chain we are as strong as the weakest link
Especially when temptation pushes us to the brink.
With God in our vessel, our ship will sure not sink.
Yet without Him, it could be gone, as quick as a wink.

GOD TEACH ME TO LOVE JUST LIKE YOU

God my Lord teach me how to love like You.
When the storms are rolling high, the sun has
Hid it's face and the sky is not blue.
God my Lord teach me how to love like You.

When everything is great
And seems so perfect and new.
God my Lord teach me how to love like You.
When the bad turns good and
The good turns bad and I don't know what to do
God my Lord teach me how to love like You.

When there are earthquake in diverse
Places and Salvation don't seem so true.
God my Lord teach me how to love like You.
When disease and death takes its toll
And for a cure we have no clue.
God my Lord teach me how to love just like You.

When truth and faith is at the gate
And I'm still going through.
God my Lord teach me how to love like You.
No matter what, where, when, how, if many, or few
God my Lord teach me to love like You.

TO MAVIS THEPATHWRITER

We are close, even though we are so far away
Another day in His presence, God has kept us to stay.
In my eyes you are a Queen even in tribulations
Because of God's love, grace and salvation.

Run with perseverance and win your race.
Mom remain in His anointing care and embrace.
God eye is on you and Pathfinder Poetry.
Continue to find your ways through Christ
And His Ministry.

CELEBRATING THE BIRTH OF CHRIST

Celebrating the birth of Christ
The birth that give us humans the rights,
To link up with God as a seed
And enjoy the blessing, as God's Word we read.

Jesus was born for us human salvation
So we can be one, back with God as His creation.
Ohh what a joy!! Ohh what a jubilee!!
The day "Jesus The Christ" was born to set us free.

PLANTING SEEDS

KAWAYNE GodisReal

Planting seeds and to see them grow
Setting them in order, what we call in a row.
Have them set according to how they ought to bear
Love, prosperity, humbleness, and God's fear.

Waiting patiently ……………….for the outcome
Not wanting to miss anything not even a crumb.
Now the time has come for them to be born
Love, prosperity, humbleness,
Godly fear will keep you from harm.

Just remember what
You put in, that is what you will get.
The best growth is when with them,
God's Word we wet.

So plant your seed with the help,
Of the Creators Hand
And He will let them manifest,
According to plan*

DO YOU KNOW JESUS ?

As I think about the question DO YOU KNOW JESUS? Tears wells up in my eyes since it brings me back to the night I accept Jesus in my heart as my personal Savior. There I was on a high rising building planning to jump and take my own life.

The bad choices, pain, and hurt have taken its toll and I did not want to live anymore. There I cried out to God and He revealed Himself to me in such an awesome way I could not deny His existence and His love for me. I surrendered to His Salvation as He leads and the only regret I have now is that I did not surrender to His love sooner since I have heard and rejected the Gospel so many times.

Well my reader probably you are saying to yourself my life is at a sweet spot, all is well and I see no need for God and what do I need to be saved from anyway? You might say I am a good person and I am fine and dandy.

No matter how good we say we are, we are **ALL** born in sin and fall short of the Glory of God (Roman 3:23). We will all die one day BAR NONE and for us to live with God in Heaven we need a Savior (which is Jesus God's Son). Heaven is real even if you think it is hocus pocus chatter, and when you think of

Heaven alternative (hell) that should make you think again.

Well if you are like I was you might be thinking I don't need Jesus now but when I am about to die I will accept Him then. But then other questions arises, do you know when you will die? Do you know how you will die? No one knows the day, and that is why God is always saying NOW today is the day for Salvation.

Tomorrow is promised to no one. If you would like to receive Jesus in your heart please pray this prayer. Lord Jesus I acknowledge that I am a sinner and I need a Savior. Please forgive me of all my sins, come and live in my heart, please cleanse me and fill me with your Holy Spirit.

If you were sincere with that prayer by believing in your heart and speaking with your mouth, you are now Born Again with the Spirit of Christ in you. Feed His Spirit with the Word of God (The Bible) and ask God to lead you to a good Bible believing Church. My contact info is at the back of this book if you would like to talk to me about your decision for Christ.

God Bless you!!

Author Contact Info

Email.....**mavisab123@gmail.com**
Or mavisab@aol.com

FB Poetry Page

Mavis "The Pathwriter" Brown

*On my poetry page are poems, poetry videos
and picture slides etc.*

Other book by Mavis ThePathWriter

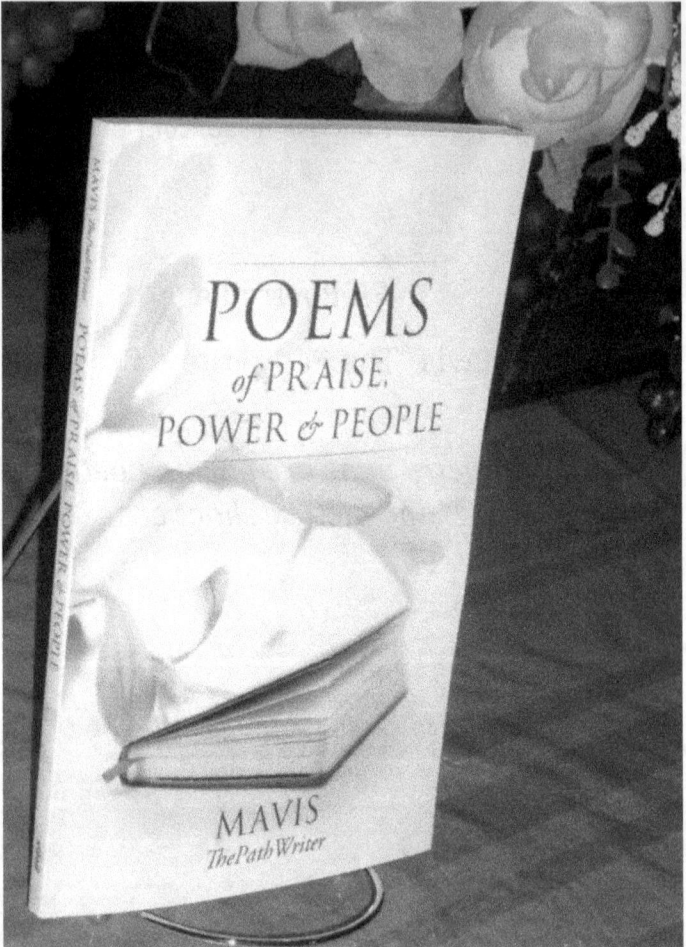

www.ingramcontent.com/pod-product-compliance
Lightning Source LLC
LaVergne TN
LVHW051132080426
835510LV00018B/2375